Training Up
a Little Guy

Inspiration *and*
Wisdom *for*
Raising Boys

HARVEST HOUSE PUBLISHERS

EUGENE, OREGON

paintings *by* *Jim Daly*

Training Up *a Little Guy*

Text copyright © 2006 by Harvest House Publishers
Eugene, Oregon 97402

ISBN-13: 978-0-7369-1801-5

Artwork © by Jim Daly and may not be reproduced without permission.

Design and Production by Koechel Peterson & Associates, Inc., Minneapolis, Minnesota

Harvest House Publishers has made every effort to trace the ownership of all poems and quotes. In the event of a question arising from the use of a poem or quote, we regret any error made and will be pleased to make the necessary correction in future editions of this book.

Unless otherwise indicated, all Scripture verses marked NIV are taken from the HOLY BIBLE, NEW INTERNATIONAL VERSION®. NIV®. Copyright©1973, 1978, 1984 by the International Bible Society. Used by permission of Zondervan. All rights reserved.

Verses marked GNT are taken from the Good News Translation – Second Edition © 1992 by American Bible Society. Used by permission.

Verses marked KJV are taken from the King James Version of the Bible.

Printed in China

10 11 12 13 14 / IM / 10 9 8 7 6

TABLE of Contents

LITTLE GUY EXPRESS COMPANY

OFFERS

TRAIN SCHEDULE

✕ Dining Car

The Train Is Now Boarding! **04**

The TRAIN Is Now BOARDING!

How satisfying it is to give a gift to a little boy! See how his eyes light up when he unwraps a shiny red fire truck or a toy train with its track. Delight in his grin when he discovers a new set of blocks waiting in the playroom. Cherish the look of surprise on his face when Dad brings home his first best friend—a frisky, tail-wagging puppy.

As enjoyable as it is to give gifts to the little guys in our lives, it's ten times more rewarding to give youngsters the gifts that last a lifetime—the life lessons that result in good character. Whether they're imparted by example, by story, or by experience, these gifts will allow a bouncing baby boy to develop one day into a man who makes good choices, helps others, and has a satisfying and rewarding life.

Childhood is a journey, one filled with learning and love, with many stations along the way. At every station stop, you can help a little guy form good character and develop strong virtues.

All aboard!

Boys are found everywhere—on top of, underneath, inside of, climbing on, swinging from, running around or jumping to. Mothers love them, little girls hate them, older sisters and brothers tolerate them, adults ignore them and Heaven protects them. A boy is Truth with dirt on its face, Beauty with a cut on its finger, Wisdom with bubble gum in its hair and the Hope of the future with a frog in its pocket.

—*"WHAT IS A BOY?"* PAMPHLET DISTRIBUTED BY THE NEW ENGLAND LIFE INSURANCE CO.

to Be ATTENTIVE

"**P**ay attention!" It's a common command, but an invaluable life lesson. Just think of what we miss when we *don't* pay attention—the beauty of the world around us, an important business detail, even dangers that would best be avoided.

When we train a little boy to be attentive, we can encourage him to study a bug just thirty seconds longer. We can gently yet firmly guide him to clean up a mess he'd rather ignore. We can read him a story, then ask a few leading questions to see if he remembered the interesting details. When we train up a little guy to be attentive, we give him the gift of discovering a fascinating, orderly world and making his own unique mark upon it.

Sons, listen to what your father teaches you.
Pay attention, and you will
have understanding.

—The book of Proverbs

Be a good listener.
Your ears will never
get you in trouble.

—Frank Tyger

To the attentive eye, each moment of the year has
its own beauty, and in the same field, it beholds,
every hour, a picture which was never seen before,
and which shall never be seen again.

—Ralph Waldo Emerson

Those who are silent, self-effacing and attentive become the recipients of confidences.

— THORNTON WILDER

Training Up
a Little Guy...

to Be OBEDiENT

When little boys are exploring their world and finding out the way things work, following the rules can be a real challenge. The urge to ask "Why?" and to question everything can sometimes turn from innocent curiosity to intentional disobedience. One is a desirable character quality; the other obviously is not.

So work with your little guy on how he can best go about understanding his world. As much as possible, let him play and explore to his heart's content. At the same time, give him the guidance he needs to stay within the boundaries. Train up his heart to obey, and the combination of curiosity and steadfast character will someday make a good man.

> *Obedience is the mother of success,*
> *and success the parent of salvation.*
>
> —Aeschylus

> *Obedience...is the primary object*
> *of all sound education.*
>
> —Elizabeth Missing Sewell

> *I have thought about it a great deal,*
> *and the more I think, the more certain*
> *I am that obedience is the gateway*
> *through which knowledge, yes, and love,*
> *too, enter the mind of the child.*
>
> —Anne Sullivan

to Be TRUThFUL

People who tell the truth earn our trust. We know they can be counted on. We give them important jobs to do. We ask for—and take—their advice. We look up to them. They are our role models, our heroes. And an honest character is developed in childhood.

Granted, little guys do like to embellish stories, to live in a world of make-believe and adventure. While it's important to honor the imaginative realm of childhood, it's essential to gently distinguish fact from fiction, to answer questions with truth and honesty. Train up a little guy to be truthful, and he will earn the respect of the world.

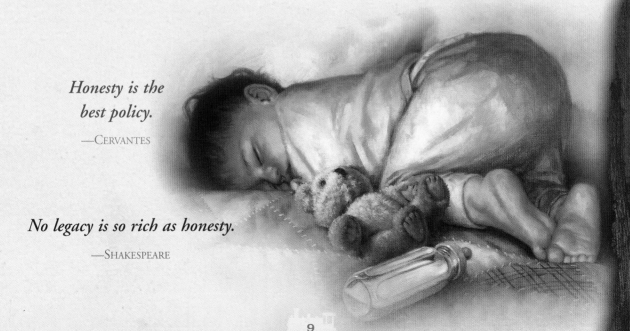

Honesty is the
best policy.

—CERVANTES

No legacy is so rich as honesty.

—SHAKESPEARE

When eating a fruit, think of the person who planted the tree.

—Vietnamese proverb

Training Up
a Little Guy...

to Be THANKFUL

"What do you say?" It's a familiar prompt from parents and caregivers to little ones. While most children truly do have thankful hearts, the all-important expression of thanks sometimes is lost in the joy of the moment. But saying "thank you" counts. It's important. Thankfulness makes the world a joyous place and builds bonds of love and respect between people.

Beyond saying "thank you" for gifts given, it's also a good idea to train children to count their blessings, to give thanks for autumn pumpkins, summer sunshine, and winter snowflakes. Little boys need to develop an appreciation for friends and family. Train up a little guy to be thankful, and you will add a generous dose of joy to the world.

A thankful heart is not only the greatest virtue, but the parent of all other virtues.

—Cicero

A single thankful thought toward heaven is the most perfect of all prayers.

—Gotthold Ephraim Lessing

Let us be grateful to people who make us happy; they are the charming gardeners who make our souls blossom.

—Marcel Proust

Training Up
a Little Guy...

to Be GENEROUS

"Mine!" It's a classic kid cry. Wouldn't it be music to your ears to hear, instead, "Mine! *And* yours!" Start small—sharing a cookie with a sibling, taking turns on a slide at the park, spending time giving the family cat positive attention—and little acts of sharing can build up to heartfelt displays of generosity.

So encourage your little one to give money to your church or a favorite charity. Model the spirit of giving in your own actions, perhaps denying yourself a treat in order to bless someone else with one. Train up a little guy to be generous, and he will be a blessing to everyone his life touches.

Generosity lies less in giving much than in giving at the right moment.
—Jean de La Bruyère

Real generosity toward the future lies in giving all to the present.
—Albert Camus

You will make all kinds of mistakes; but as long as you are generous and true, and also fierce, you cannot hurt the world or even seriously distress her. She was made to be wooed and won by youth.
—Sir Winston Churchill

Thoughtfulness for others, generosity, modesty, and self-respect, are all the qualities which make a real gentleman...as distinguished from the veneered article which commonly goes by that name.
—Thomas Huxley

Order is Heav'n's first law.
—ALEXANDER POPE

Training Up
a Little Guy...

to Be ORDeRLY

Small, muddy boot prints making a winding trail throughout the entire house. Cookie crumbs on a plate and milk drops in a glass. Plastic figures stuck in play dough, and rescue vehicles in the flower beds. Such are the signs that a little boy inhabits this household.

Although life with children means letting some things go, it doesn't mean you need to declare your dwelling a disaster area. Little by little, you can train your whirling dervish to put his dishes by the sink, pick up his toys, and leave his muddy shoes on the porch. The world is a place of creativity, but it's also a place of order. "A place for everything and everything in its place" are good words to live by. Train up your little guy to be orderly, and you'll give him a gift he can take into his own home one day.

Neatness begets order.

—JOHANN KASPAR LAVATER

If you chase two rabbits, both will escape.

—TRADITIONAL SAYING

*Soon, in all parts of our country, in each neglected village,
or new settlement, the Christian female teacher will quietly
take her station, collecting the ignorant children around her,
teaching them habits of neatness, order and thrift; opening
the book of knowledge, inspiring the principles of morality,
and awakening the hope of immortality.*

—CATHERINE BEECHER

Training Up
a Little Guy...

to Be FORGIVING

It's a fact of life. Little kids will drop and break dishes. They will get into other people's things—and sometimes they'll ruin them. They will get frustrated with siblings and call them names. Whether accidental or intentional, kids will make mistakes.

Grown-ups will make mistakes, too. They'll blame the wrong child, or they'll be short-tempered after a hard day's work. And while we can't erase words spoken in anger or fix a broken glass, the art of forgiveness is a virtue worth nurturing. *I'm sorry. Please forgive me. I didn't mean to. I'll try to do better next time.* Train up a little guy to be forgiving, and you'll train him to have an honest and humble heart—one that puts genuine effort into making things all right again.

We reflected
If one by one we counted people out
For the least sin, it wouldn't take us long
To get so we had no one left to live with,
For to be social is to be forgiving.

—ROBERT FROST

Pray you now, forget and forgive.

—SHAKESPEARE

Good, to forgive;
Best, to forget!

—ROBERT BROWNING

Good nature and good sense must ever join;
To err is human, to forgive divine.

—ALEXANDER POPE

Forgive others whenever you can.

—CHINESE PROVERB

Training Up
a Little Guy...
to Be RESPONSIBLE

Responsible people earn our trust. They're the ones we call upon when help is needed. They take on the difficult jobs—and they see them through to completion. Responsible people are willing to be put in charge. Responsible people make good things happen.

You can begin cultivating the gift of responsibility in a little boy at a very young age. Let him know what your expectations are, then show him you are confident he can follow through. Encourage him to help others. Give him tasks that will stretch and challenge him—and express your excitement when he comes through! Train up a little guy to be responsible, and you will help to develop a strong leader with a heart for service.

The one quality that all successful people have is the ability to take on responsibility.
—MICHAEL KORDA

The price of greatness is responsibility.
—SIR WINSTON CHURCHILL

If you want your children to keep their feet on the ground, put some responsibility on their shoulders.
—ABIGAIL VAN BUREN

Training Up *a Little Guy...*

to Be PATIENT

Waiting and children go together like oil and water. Vacations, holidays, special occasions—it's so hard for children to be patient. Think of a car trip: "Are we there *yet?*" Or a birthday: "*How* many days till I'm six?" Even waiting for you to get off the phone so you can play together can be excruciating for a young child!

Yet patience *is* truly a virtue. Patient people have less worry and anxiety in their lives. They can entertain themselves in the meantime. They give a sense of calmness to a group of people. So begin to build patience in your little guy. Help him in tangible ways. Make a paper chain to count off the days until a much-anticipated holiday. Give him something to do while you talk on the phone. Train up a little guy to be patient, and you will help him to be a calm, reliable person who brings peace to his world.

He who knows patience knows peace.

—CHINESE PROVERB

Patience is the best remedy for every trouble.

—PLAUTUS

Patience is a necessary ingredient of genius.

—BENJAMIN DISRAELI

He that has patience may compass anything.

—FRANÇOIS RABELAIS

Training Up *a Little Guy...*
to Be SELF-CONTROLLED

But my feet didn't *mean* to kick my brother!" "My hand just couldn't *help* but draw on the walls!" "I didn't *think* that would hurt my sister's doll!" "My mouth ate that cookie all on its own!" Little hands and little feet sometimes don't do what their owner knows in his heart is right. It's hard to have self-control when someone angers you or when a forbidden activity (or cookie!) looks oh-so-tempting.

Yet imagine a world in which nobody possessed the virtue of self-control. We already see enough evidence of such a world today. Do we really need to see any more? Little boys who are self-controlled turn into men who know how to deal with difficult emotions and feelings in a positive, peaceful way. Train up a little guy to be self-controlled, and you will give him the tools to lead a life that helps instead of harms others as well as himself.

Self-reverence, self-knowledge,
self-control,—These three alone
lead life to sovereign power.

—ALFRED, LORD TENNYSON

Mental toughness is many things and rather
difficult to explain. Its qualities are sacrifice
and self-denial...It's a state of mind—
you could call it character in action.

—VINCE LOMBARDI

20

Training Up *a Little Guy...*

to Be CREATIVE

When we think of creativity, the image of a great painter, a talented musician, or a captivating author usually springs to mind. But creativity can manifest itself in many ways. Engineers, teachers, and cabinetmakers can all use their creative gifts to bless the world.

Perhaps the best way to help children develop their creative powers is to give them the gift of time. Let a little boy spend hours playing with Legos. Provide a hammer, nails, and an unlimited supply of scrap wood. Reams of paper and colored pencils keep some children occupied for hours. Add a hearty dose of encouragement, and you have a budding artist—in his own unique way. Train up a little guy to be creative, and you will put him on the path to using his gifts, talents, and skills while creating his own unique masterpiece.

All children have creative power.

—Brenda Ueland

If You Want to Write (1938)

We are all of us imaginative in some form or other.

—George Eliot

Creative force, like a musical composer, goes on unweariedly repeating a simple air or theme, now high, now low, in solo, in chorus, ten thousand times reverberated, till it fills earth and heaven with the chant.

—Ralph Waldo Emerson

Training Up
a Little Guy...

to Be DILIGENT

Stick-to-itiveness. Stamina. Steadfastness. No matter what you call it, diligence is a most helpful character trait. Good athletes, good businessmen, and good parents all need it. A diligent person may not be the fastest or the most gifted at completing a task, but he has one advantage over someone who lacks the gift of diligence: He will get the job done. And his strong work ethic will result in increased skill and confidence.

You can start developing a child's diligent character early on in life. Encourage a little boy to finish out a project to its completion. If a block tower starts to topple, don't get frustrated. Help him build a bigger and better one. If he can't kick a soccer ball very far or if learning to ride a bike seems to be an insurmountable challenge, encourage him not to give up—and don't give up on him, either. Keep working together. It doesn't matter how long it takes. Train up a little guy to be diligent, and you will give him the ability to accomplish much in life.

Diligence is a priceless treasure...

—CHINESE PROVERB

Consider the postage stamp:
Its usefulness consists in the ability
to stick to one thing til it gets there.

—JOSH BILLINGS

The best strategy in life is diligence.

—TRADITIONAL SAYING

The leading rule for the lawyer, as for the man of every other calling, is diligence.
Leave nothing for to-morrow which can be done to-day.

—ABRAHAM LINCOLN

*Great riches come
from heaven;
small riches come
from diligence.*

—CHINESE PROVERB

An ounce of loyalty is worth a pound of cleverness.

—ELBERT HUBBARD

Training Up
a Little Guy...

to Be LOYAL *and* LOVING

Loyalty builds strong families, strong communities, strong countries. Combine loyalty with love and you have a combination that can change the world for good. When children are raised in a positive, loving environment, they learn how best to go about doing what is right for the right person or the right cause.

Start within the family—parents, brothers, sisters. Celebrate each other's accomplishments. Encourage and pray for each other. Then expand outward—grandparents, cousins, friends, neighbors, classmates. Stick up for others. Perform small acts of kindness. Plan good surprises. Train up a little guy to be loyal and loving, and he will be a shining beacon of light for all that is good in the world.

Nobody wishes bad manners.
We must have loyalty and character.

—RALPH WALDO EMERSON

Love is not blind—it sees more, not less.
But because it sees more,
it is willing to see less.

—JULIUS GORDON

There are loyal hearts, there are spirits brave,
There are souls that are pure and true;
Then give to the world the best you have,
And the best will come back to you.

—MADELINE BRIDGES

Training Up
a Little Guy...

to Be DETERMINED

Determination in a small child can be a daunting thing. *Stubborn. Bullheaded. Aggressive.* The words used to describe a determined little one usually have negative connotations. So try changing your thinking. Dwell on the positives. He's persistent. He doesn't give up. He really wants to make things work.

Bit by bit, show this little guy that some things are good to go after. And teach him that sometimes it's not okay to press on. Be consistent with things like bedtime, mealtime, and expectations for proper behavior. Choose your battles wisely, give encouragement for positive shows of persistence, and gently and firmly refuse to give in to negative determination. Train up a little guy to be determined, and he'll be ready to take on the world—in a positive way.

If one has determination,
then things will get done.
—CHINESE PROVERB

He only is a well-made man who
has a good determination.
—RALPH WALDO EMERSON

Persistence can grind an iron beam down into a needle.
—CHINESE PROVERB

*Nothing in the world can take
the place of Persistence.
Talent will not; nothing is
more common than
unsuccessful men with talent.
Genius will not; unrewarded
genius is almost a proverb.
Education will not; the world
is full of educated derelicts.
Persistence and Determination
alone are omnipotent.
The slogan "Press On,"
has solved and will always
solve the problems of
the human race.*

—Calvin Coolidge

*Loving parents
have caring
children.*
—PROVERB

to Be COMPASSIONATE

Compassion is one of those virtues that is often underemphasized—and sometimes even neglected—in a little boy's upbringing. Yet our world is in need of compassionate women *and* men. Compassionate people meet the needs of others. They truly do love their neighbor as themselves.

Like all virtues, compassion needs to be modeled. When little boys get hurt, it's tempting to tell them to be brave and stoic, not to cry. But they do get hurt. How much time does it take to bestow a quick look, a gentle kiss, and a favorite Band-Aid? The time spent is minimal, but the investment is lasting. From there, teach a boy how to console and care for others. Train up a little guy to be compassionate, and he will one day become a caring father and friend.

True kindness presupposes the faculty
of imagining as one's own
the suffering and joys of others.

—André Gide

Real kindness seeks no return;
What return can the world
make to rain clouds?

—Tiruvalluvar

The words of kindness are more healing to a drooping heart than balm or honey.

—Sarah Fielding

While he was still a long way off, his father saw him and was filled with compassion
for him; he ran to his son, threw his arms around him and kissed him.

—The Book of Luke

Training Up
a Little Guy...

to Be WISE

Wisdom goes beyond getting good grades, scoring high on I.Q. tests, or being labeled as "gifted." Those who are truly wise make good decisions. They're able to see the "big picture." They have the gift of reason and the ability to truly evaluate a situation—and then to make the correct choice about what to do.

When you teach a child wisdom, start small. Perhaps the most important starting point is to teach that a person's actions have consequences. If you choose to be rough with your toys, they break. If you choose to treat a friend unkindly, you'll need to spend time alone in your room. If you don't eat your dinner, you must not have room for dessert. Wise adults also realize that they are models for children. Kids need an example to follow, so make wise choices. Train up a little guy to be wise, and he will be a truly intelligent thinker who makes the right choices in life.

With the ancient is wisdom, and in length of days understanding.

—THE BOOK OF JOB

We teach boys to be such men as we are. We do not teach them to aspire to be all they can. We do not give them a training as if we believed in their noble nature. We scarce educate their bodies. We do not train the eye and the hand. We exercise their understandings to the apprehension and comparison of some facts, to a skill in numbers, in words; we aim to make accountants, attorneys, engineers; but not to make able, earnest, great-hearted men.

—RALPH WALDO EMERSON

And wisdom is
a butterfly…
—WILLIAM BUTLER YEATS

A wise man hears one word and understands two.
—YIDDISH PROVERB

Wisdom is the principal thing; therefore get wisdom:
and with all thy getting get understanding.
—THE BOOK OF PROVERBS

To be a man is…to be responsible. It is to feel shame at the sight of what seems to be unmerited misery. It is to take pride in a victory won by one's comrades. It is to feel, when setting one's stone, that one is contributing to the building of the world.

—ANTOINE DE SAINT EXUPÉRY

Great difficulties may be surmounted by patience and perseverance.

—ABIGAIL ADAMS

It is not enough to have great qualities. We should also have the management of them.

—LA ROCHEFOUCAULD

[The children] live in a world of delightful imagination; they pursue persons and objects that never existed; they make an Argosy laden with gold out of a floating butterfly…

—WOODROW WILSON

That best portion of a good man's life, His little, nameless, unremembered acts Of kindness and of love.

—WILLIAM WORDSWORTH